Mastering Content Creation with ChatGPT

C. P. Kumar
Reiki Healer
Roorkee - 247667, India

DEDICATION

To all content creators and aspiring writers,

This book is dedicated to you. It is a tribute to your passion, creativity, and hard work in shaping the digital world through the power of words. "Mastering Content Creation with ChatGPT" is a comprehensive guide that explores the limitless possibilities of using ChatGPT, a state-of-the-art language model, for content creation.

Through the 16 chapters of this book, we have provided a detailed and practical roadmap for using ChatGPT to create engaging, informative, and high-quality content across various domains, including social media, blogging, email marketing, copywriting, academic research, fiction, product descriptions, chatbots, video scripts, and technical documentation.

We acknowledge the fact that ChatGPT is not a replacement for human creativity and expertise. Instead, it is a tool that can enhance your skills and provide a fresh perspective on your content creation process. We have also discussed the ethical considerations involved in using ChatGPT and emphasized the importance of responsible usage.

As you embark on this journey of mastering content creation with ChatGPT, we hope that this book will serve as a valuable resource and inspire you to push the boundaries of your creativity. May your words continue to captivate, educate, and entertain the world.

C. P. Kumar

CONTENTS

PREFACE

In today's fast-paced digital world, content creation is essential for businesses, marketers, writers, and creators of all kinds. However, producing high-quality and engaging content consistently can be challenging and time-consuming. This is where ChatGPT, a large language model trained by OpenAI, comes in.

ChatGPT is an AI tool that can generate human-like text based on the input provided. Its capabilities are vast and versatile, making it a valuable asset for content creators. This book aims to guide readers on how to master content creation with ChatGPT.

This book is designed to provide a comprehensive understanding of ChatGPT and its applications in various content creation contexts. It includes chapters that cover a wide range of topics, from social media content creation to technical documentation generation.

In the first chapter, readers will be introduced to ChatGPT and its capabilities. This will provide a foundation for understanding how the tool works and what it can do. The subsequent chapters focus on specific content creation contexts and how ChatGPT can be used effectively in each of these contexts.

The book is written with a practical approach, providing step-by-step instructions, tips, and tricks for using ChatGPT. Each chapter is designed to be standalone, so readers can easily skip to the relevant section that interests them.

The final chapter of the book covers ethical considerations when using ChatGPT for content creation. It is crucial to understand the ethical implications of AI-generated content and ensure that it is used responsibly and with integrity.

Overall, this book is a comprehensive guide for anyone looking to master content creation with ChatGPT. Whether you are a writer, marketer, or content creator of any kind, this book will provide you with the tools and knowledge you need to take your content creation to the next level.

C. P. Kumar

Reiki Healer

Former Scientist 'G', National Institute of Hydrology
Roorkee - 247667, India
E-mail: cpkumar@yahoo.com
Web: https://www.angelfire.com/nh/cpkumar/virgo.html

Introduction

ChatGPT is a powerful AI-based chatbot that can understand natural language inputs and respond accordingly. It is based on the GPT-3.5 architecture, which is a deep learning model that can generate human-like text responses. ChatGPT is one of the most advanced chatbots available today, and it has a wide range of capabilities that make it suitable for a variety of use cases. In this article, we will introduce ChatGPT and its capabilities, as well as provide a step-by-step guide and tips and tricks for using it effectively.

What is ChatGPT?

ChatGPT is an advanced language model designed by OpenAI, based on the GPT-3.5 architecture. It is a state-of-the-art natural language processing model that uses deep learning algorithms to understand and generate human-like responses to text-based inputs. ChatGPT has been trained on vast amounts of text data from various sources, including books, articles, and websites, allowing it to learn the nuances of language and context.

With its advanced algorithms, ChatGPT can understand and generate text in multiple languages, making it an incredibly versatile tool for communication and problem-solving. It can converse on a wide range of topics, from news and current events to science, history, and entertainment, and can even generate creative writing such as poetry and short stories. ChatGPT's ability to understand human language and respond in a human-like manner makes it an excellent tool for customer service, education, and research, as it can quickly provide information and respond to queries with accuracy and speed.

Capabilities of ChatGPT

ChatGPT has a number of capabilities that make it stand out from other chatbots. Some of the key capabilities include:

1. Natural Language Processing (NLP): ChatGPT is capable of understanding natural language inputs and responding accordingly. It can handle a wide range of inputs, including questions, statements, and commands.

2. Conversational AI: ChatGPT is designed to be a conversational AI that can engage in a back-and-forth dialogue with users. It is capable of understanding context and providing relevant responses based on the conversation.

3. Knowledge Base: ChatGPT has access to a large knowledge base that it can draw upon to provide answers to users' questions. This knowledge base includes a wide range of topics, from general knowledge to specialized subjects.

4. Personalization: ChatGPT is capable of learning from user interactions and personalizing its responses accordingly. It can remember previous conversations and tailor its responses to individual users.

5. Multi-lingual Support: ChatGPT is capable of supporting multiple languages, making it suitable for use in a global context.

Step-by-Step Guide for Using ChatGPT

Using ChatGPT is easy and straightforward. Here is a step-by-step guide for getting started:

Step 1: Access ChatGPT

The first step is to access ChatGPT. You can do this by visiting the OpenAI website or using one of the third-party chatbot platforms that integrate with ChatGPT.

Step 2: Initiate a Conversation

Once you have accessed ChatGPT, you can initiate a conversation by typing in a message. ChatGPT will respond with a greeting and prompt you to provide more information.

Step 3: Ask Questions or Provide Statements

You can then ask questions or provide statements to ChatGPT. It is important to be clear and concise in your messages to ensure that ChatGPT understands your intent.

Step 4: Engage in Dialogue

ChatGPT is designed to engage in a back-and-forth dialogue with users. You can continue the conversation by responding to ChatGPT's messages and asking follow-up questions.

Step 5: Provide Feedback

ChatGPT is constantly learning and improving based on user interactions. If you notice that ChatGPT is not providing accurate responses, you can provide feedback to help it improve.

Tips and Tricks for Using ChatGPT

Here are some tips and tricks for using ChatGPT effectively:

1. Be Clear and Concise: When communicating with ChatGPT, it is important to be clear and concise in your messages. Avoid using complex language or vague statements that could lead to misunderstandings.

2. Ask Specific Questions: ChatGPT is designed to provide answers to specific questions. When asking questions, try to be as specific as possible to help ChatGPT understand your intent.

3. Provide Context: Providing context can help ChatGPT understand the intent behind your messages. For example, if you are asking about a particular product, provide information about the product to help ChatGPT provide accurate responses.

4. Use Keywords: Using relevant keywords in your messages can help ChatGPT understand your intent and provide more accurate responses.

5. Provide Feedback: Providing feedback to ChatGPT is important as it helps the AI model improve its responses over time. If you notice that ChatGPT is not providing accurate or helpful responses, you can provide feedback by using the feedback feature in the chatbot interface.

6. Experiment with Different Phrasing: ChatGPT can understand a variety of phrasing and language

structures. If you are not getting the desired response, try rephrasing your question or statement in a different way.

7. Use the Knowledge Base: ChatGPT has access to a large knowledge base that it can draw upon to provide answers to your questions. Before asking a question, try searching the knowledge base to see if there is already an answer available.

8. Personalize the Conversation: ChatGPT can learn from previous interactions and personalize its responses accordingly. If you are a returning user, ChatGPT may remember your previous conversation and use that information to provide more personalized responses.

9. Stay Safe: ChatGPT is a powerful tool, but it is important to remember that it is still an AI model and may not always provide accurate information. Be cautious when using ChatGPT to make important decisions and always double-check information provided by the chatbot.

Limitations of ChatGPT: Understanding What It Can and Cannot Do

As an AI language model, ChatGPT is a powerful tool for generating text, answering questions, and providing information on a wide range of topics. However, there are certain limitations to what ChatGPT can do. One of these limitations is that its knowledge cutoff date is September 2021, which means that it may not be able to provide information on events or developments that have occurred since then. Additionally, ChatGPT cannot provide real-time information or news updates, as it is not connected to live data feeds or news sources.

Another limitation of ChatGPT is that it cannot forecast weather or predict future events or outcomes with high accuracy. While it may be able to provide some general information or trends based on past data, it cannot make accurate predictions about specific events or situations. Similarly, ChatGPT cannot suggest the "best" items or things, as this is often a subjective judgment that depends on individual preferences and needs.

Despite these limitations, ChatGPT remains a valuable tool for generating text and providing information on a wide range of topics. Its ability to understand and generate natural language makes it a powerful resource for language-related tasks such as translation, summarization, and question-answering. However, it is important to recognize the limitations of ChatGPT and use it appropriately for the tasks it is best suited for.

Conclusion

ChatGPT is a powerful AI-based chatbot that has a wide range of capabilities, including natural language processing, conversational AI, a knowledge base, personalization, and multi-lingual support. Using ChatGPT is easy and straightforward, and there are a number of tips and tricks that can help you use it effectively. By following the step-by-step guide and implementing the tips and tricks provided in this article, you can get the most out of ChatGPT and improve your interactions with the AI model.

Introduction

In today's digital age, social media has become an indispensable part of our lives. The use of social media platforms has increased significantly over the years, with more people engaging with it for various purposes. One of the main reasons why people use social media is to post and share content. Whether it's a personal blog, a brand's marketing campaign, or simply sharing content for fun, social media has become a popular platform for content distribution.

However, creating content for social media is not always an easy task. It can be time-consuming and require a lot of effort and creativity. This is where ChatGPT comes in. ChatGPT is an artificial intelligence language model that can help with social media content creation. In this article, we will explore how ChatGPT can be used for social media content generation and its benefits.

How can ChatGPT be used for social media content creation?

ChatGPT can be used for various social media content creation tasks. Some of the most common ones are:

1. Content generation: ChatGPT can be used to generate social media content, such as blog posts, social media captions, and tweets. It can help save time and effort by generating content ideas, headlines, and even the body of the text.

2. Content optimization: ChatGPT can be used to optimize social media content by suggesting improvements, such as better keywords, hashtags, and formatting.

3. Content curation: ChatGPT can be used to curate content by suggesting articles, videos, and images that are relevant to a particular topic or audience.

4. Content analysis: ChatGPT can be used to analyze social media content by identifying trends, sentiment, and other insights that can be used to improve content strategy.

Benefits of using ChatGPT for social media content creation

1. Time-saving: Creating social media content can be time-consuming, especially if you have to do it on a regular basis. ChatGPT can help save time by generating content ideas, headlines, and even the body of the text. This can help free up time that can be used for other tasks.

2. Consistency: ChatGPT can help maintain consistency in social media content creation by generating content that is relevant to a particular brand or audience. This can help maintain the brand's tone and style across different social media platforms.

3. Creativity: ChatGPT can help spark creativity by generating content ideas that are unique and relevant to a particular topic or audience. This can help create content that is engaging and can stand out in a crowded social media space.

4. Cost-effective: Hiring a social media content creator can be expensive, especially for small businesses or individuals. ChatGPT can help reduce the cost of content creation by generating content that is of high quality and relevant to a particular brand or audience.

5. Data-driven insights: ChatGPT can help provide data-driven insights into social media content by analyzing trends, sentiment, and other metrics. This can help improve content strategy and ensure that it resonates with the target audience.

Limitations of using ChatGPT for social media content creation

1. Lack of human touch: ChatGPT can generate human-like text, but it still lacks the human touch that is required for social media content creation. Social media content is not just about the text, but also the visuals, tone, and style. ChatGPT may not be able to fully capture these elements, which may result in content that is not engaging or does not align with the brand's values.

2. Limited creativity: While ChatGPT can help spark creativity, it may not be able to generate truly unique content ideas. This is because it is trained on a massive corpus of data, which means that it may generate content that is similar to what already exists online.

3. Quality issues: ChatGPT may generate content that is grammatically correct and coherent, but it may not always be of high quality. It may miss nuances or cultural references that are important for social media content creation.

4. Limited customization: ChatGPT generates content based on the input provided to it. While it may provide suggestions for optimization, it may not be able to fully customize content to suit a particular brand or audience.

How to use ChatGPT for social media content creation

Using ChatGPT for social media content creation is relatively easy. Here are some steps to follow:

1. Determine the content type: Decide on the type of social media content that you want to create, such as blog posts, social media captions, or tweets.

2. Input the topic: Input the topic or keyword that you want to generate content for.

3. Review the suggestions: ChatGPT will generate content suggestions based on the input provided. Review the suggestions and select the one that is most relevant.

4. Customize the content: Customize the content to suit the brand's tone and style.

5. Review and edit: Review the content and edit it to ensure that it is of high quality and free of errors.

6. Publish: Publish the content on the appropriate social media platform.

Conclusion

ChatGPT can be a valuable tool for social media content creation. It can help save time, maintain consistency, and provide data-driven insights. However, it is important to recognize its limitations and ensure that the content generated is of high quality and aligns with the brand's values. ChatGPT can be used as a supplement to human creativity and expertise, but it should not replace it entirely. With proper use and customization, ChatGPT can be an effective tool for social media content creation.

Introduction

In today's digital age, content creation has become more important than ever before. With the rise of social media and the internet, businesses and individuals alike are constantly seeking new and creative ways to engage with their audience. Blogging is one of the most popular ways to achieve this, but coming up with fresh and engaging ideas can be a challenge. This is where ChatGPT comes in. As a large language model, ChatGPT can help you generate unique and exciting blog post ideas and even assist in the writing process. In this article, we will explore how to use ChatGPT for blog post ideas and writing.

Generating Blog Post Ideas with ChatGPT

One of the biggest challenges when it comes to blogging is coming up with fresh and engaging ideas. ChatGPT can help you overcome this challenge by generating a list of potential topics to write about. Here's how:

Step 1: Start by providing ChatGPT with a general topic or keyword related to your blog niche. For example, if your blog is about travel, you could provide the prompt "travel".

Step 2: ChatGPT will then generate a list of related topics. You can use these topics as inspiration for your blog posts. For example, ChatGPT might suggest "best places to visit in Europe", "budget travel tips", or "how to pack for a backpacking trip".

Step 3: Review the list of topics generated by ChatGPT and select the ones that you find most interesting or relevant to your blog. You can then use these topics as the basis for your blog posts.

Writing with ChatGPT

Once you have a topic in mind, ChatGPT can also assist you with the writing process. Here's how:

Step 1: Start by providing ChatGPT with a brief outline of your blog post. This could include the main points you want to cover, the tone you want to use, and any specific keywords or phrases you want to include.

Step 2: ChatGPT will then generate a draft of your blog post based on the information you provided. The draft will be written in natural language and will include suggestions for how to expand on your outline.

Step 3: Review the draft generated by ChatGPT and make any necessary edits or revisions. You can also use the draft as a starting point for your own writing.

Tips for Using ChatGPT for Blogging

While ChatGPT can be a powerful tool for generating blog post ideas and assisting with writing, there are a few tips to keep in mind:

1. Be specific with your prompts: The more specific you are with your prompts, the more accurate and relevant the output from ChatGPT will be. For example, instead of using the prompt "food", try "vegan recipes for summer BBQs".

2. Use the right tone: ChatGPT can generate text in a variety of tones, from informative to humorous. Make sure you specify the tone you want to use in your prompt to ensure that the output matches your intended style.

3. Edit and revise: While ChatGPT can generate high-quality text, it is still important to edit and revise your blog posts to ensure they are polished and error-free.

4. Use ChatGPT as a starting point: While ChatGPT can assist with writing, it should not replace your own creativity and unique voice. Use the output generated by ChatGPT as a starting point for your own writing and add your own ideas, examples, and personal touch to make your blog posts stand out.

5. Use multiple prompts: Don't rely on a single prompt to generate all of your blog post ideas. Experiment with different prompts and keywords to generate a wide variety of topics.

6. Keep your audience in mind: When using ChatGPT to generate blog post ideas and writing, it's important to keep your audience in mind. Make sure the topics and tone of your blog posts are relevant and engaging for your target audience.

7. Stay organized: As you generate blog post ideas and drafts with ChatGPT, it can be helpful to keep track of them in a document or spreadsheet. This will make it easier to plan out your content calendar and ensure that you don't forget any of the ideas generated by ChatGPT.

Conclusion

ChatGPT can be a valuable tool for bloggers looking to generate fresh and engaging content. By using prompts and outlines, you can generate a wide variety of blog post ideas and even receive assistance with the writing process. However, it's important to remember that ChatGPT should be used as a starting point and not a replacement for your own creativity and unique voice. With these tips in mind, you can use ChatGPT to take your blogging to the next level and keep your audience engaged with high-quality content.

Chapter 4. Creating engaging email subject lines with ChatGPT

Introduction

Email marketing can be a powerful tool for businesses to reach out to potential and existing customers. However, with the average person receiving dozens of emails every day, it's important to create subject lines that stand out and grab their attention. This is where ChatGPT comes in - a language model that can help you create engaging email subject lines that will increase your open rates and ultimately, your conversions.

Using ChatGPT to create engaging email subject lines

Creating an engaging email subject line is crucial to the success of your email marketing campaign. If your subject line is boring or uninteresting, your email is likely to be ignored or even deleted without being opened. However, coming up with a catchy and attention-grabbing subject line is not always easy. This is where ChatGPT can help.

Here are some tips on how to use ChatGPT to create engaging email subject lines:

1. Keep it short and sweet

One of the most important things to remember when creating an email subject line is to keep it short and sweet. Your subject line should be concise and to the point, so that it can be easily read and understood by your audience. ChatGPT can help you come up with short and catchy subject lines that will grab your audience's attention.

2. Use numbers and statistics

Using numbers and statistics in your subject line can be a great way to capture your audience's attention. People are naturally drawn to numbers, and using them in your subject line can make your email stand out from the rest. ChatGPT can help you come up with interesting and attention-grabbing statistics to include in your subject line.

3. Personalize your subject line

Personalizing your subject line can make a big difference in how your audience responds to your email. Using their name or other personal information can make them feel valued and important, and can increase the chances of them opening and engaging with your email. ChatGPT can help you come up with personalized subject lines that will resonate with your audience.

4. Create a sense of urgency

Creating a sense of urgency in your subject line can be a great way to get your audience to take action. Using phrases like "limited time offer" or "don't miss out" can make your audience feel like they need to act quickly in order to take advantage of what you're offering. ChatGPT can help you come up with urgent and compelling subject lines that will encourage your audience to take action.

5. Use humor

Using humor in your subject line can be a great way to make your email stand out and grab your audience's attention. People are naturally drawn to humor, and using it in your subject line can make your email more memorable and engaging. ChatGPT can help you come up with humorous subject lines that will make your audience laugh and want to engage with your email.

Examples of engaging email subject lines generated by ChatGPT

Here are some examples of engaging email subject lines that were generated by ChatGPT:

1. "Get 50% off your next purchase - but hurry, this offer won't last long!"
2. "You're invited to our exclusive VIP sale - don't miss out!"
3. "Personalized just for you - [Name], check out our latest products!"
4. "5 reasons why our product is the best on the market"
5. "Don't let this opportunity slip away - sign up now and save!"
6. "Get ready to laugh - our new product will knock your socks off!"

Conclusion

Using ChatGPT to create engaging email subject lines can be a powerful tool for businesses looking to increase their open rates and ultimately, their conversions. By following these tips and using ChatGPT to generate attention-grabbing subject lines, you can create emails that stand out from the rest and get your audience to take action. With ChatGPT's ability to generate human-like text, the possibilities are endless for creating engaging and effective email subject lines.

Chapter 5. ChatGPT for copywriting and marketing content

Introduction

As the digital world evolves, the demand for quality copywriting and marketing content continues to increase. The ability to create compelling and persuasive content that connects with an audience is a skill that has become essential for any business to succeed in today's competitive market. One of the emerging technologies that is rapidly changing the game for content creators is ChatGPT, an artificial intelligence-powered language model developed by OpenAI. In this article, we will explore the capabilities of ChatGPT and how it can be utilized for copywriting and marketing content.

How does ChatGPT work?

ChatGPT works by utilizing a technique called "unsupervised learning." This means that the AI model is trained on a massive amount of data without any specific direction or guidance. This allows the AI to learn patterns and relationships within the data on its own, without the need for human input.

To generate content, ChatGPT requires a prompt or a starting point in the form of a sentence or a paragraph. The prompt can be a simple question or a more complex statement that requires a detailed response. Once a prompt is entered, ChatGPT uses its vast database of knowledge to generate a response that is grammatically correct, coherent, and relevant to the topic at hand.

ChatGPT can also be fine-tuned to a specific domain or topic by training it on a dataset that is relevant to that domain. This allows it to generate more accurate and relevant content for that particular domain, making it an ideal tool for copywriting and marketing content.

Benefits of using ChatGPT for copywriting and marketing content

1. Saves time and effort

One of the primary benefits of using ChatGPT for copywriting and marketing content is that it saves a significant amount of time and effort. Writing high-quality content that is persuasive and engaging can be a time-consuming and challenging task. With ChatGPT, businesses can generate content quickly and easily, without the need for human input.

2. Improves content quality

Another significant benefit of using ChatGPT is that it improves the quality of the content. ChatGPT is trained on a massive corpus of text data, which means that it has a vast knowledge base to draw from. This allows it to generate content that is accurate, relevant, and engaging, making it an ideal tool for creating high-quality content.

3. Increases productivity

ChatGPT can significantly increase productivity for businesses that rely on content creation for their marketing strategies. With ChatGPT, businesses can generate a high volume of content quickly and easily, allowing them to focus on other aspects of their business.

4. Cost-effective

Using ChatGPT for copywriting and marketing content can be a cost-effective solution for businesses. Hiring professional writers or content creators can be expensive, especially for small businesses with limited budgets. With ChatGPT, businesses can generate high-quality content at a fraction of the cost.

5. Consistency in tone and style

ChatGPT can be trained to mimic a specific tone and style, making it an ideal tool for maintaining consistency in brand messaging. This ensures that all content generated by ChatGPT is consistent in tone and style, regardless of the person who inputs the prompt.

How to use ChatGPT for copywriting and marketing content

1. Determine the topic and goals

The first step in using ChatGPT for copywriting and marketing content is to determine the topic and goals of the content you want to generate. This can include the target audience, the purpose of the content, and the desired outcome. By identifying these key factors, you can provide ChatGPT with a clear direction on what type of content you want to generate.

2. Craft a prompt

Once you have identified the topic and goals of the content, the next step is to craft a prompt for ChatGPT. The prompt should be a clear and concise statement or question that provides ChatGPT with the necessary information to generate the desired content. It's essential to be specific with your prompt, as this will help ChatGPT to generate content that is relevant and accurate.

3. Fine-tune ChatGPT

ChatGPT can be fine-tuned to a specific domain or topic by training it on a dataset that is relevant to that domain. This can improve the accuracy and relevance of the content generated by ChatGPT. Fine-tuning ChatGPT requires some technical expertise, but there are several online tools and services available that can help with this process.

4. Evaluate and edit the generated content

Once ChatGPT has generated the content, it's essential to evaluate and edit it to ensure that it meets the desired quality and tone. While ChatGPT can generate high-quality content, it's still an AI-powered tool and may require some editing to ensure that it's coherent and engaging.

5. Use ChatGPT in conjunction with human input

While ChatGPT can be an excellent tool for generating content quickly and easily, it's important to use it in conjunction with human input. Human input can help to provide context and ensure that the content is aligned with the overall marketing strategy and brand messaging.

Examples of using ChatGPT for copywriting and marketing content

1. Social media posts

Social media posts require a consistent and engaging tone to be effective. ChatGPT can be used to generate social media posts quickly and easily, allowing businesses to maintain a consistent posting schedule. For example, a business can input a prompt like "Create a social media post about our new product launch." ChatGPT can then generate a post that is aligned with the brand messaging and includes relevant information about the product launch.

2. Product descriptions

Product descriptions are critical for eCommerce businesses. They need to be accurate, engaging, and persuasive to encourage customers to make a purchase. ChatGPT can be used to generate product descriptions quickly and easily, saving businesses time and effort. For example, a business can input a prompt like "Write a product description for our new line of shoes." ChatGPT can then generate a product description that includes details about the features and benefits of the shoes.

3. Email marketing campaigns

Email marketing campaigns require a consistent tone and style to be effective. ChatGPT can be used to generate email content quickly and easily, allowing businesses to maintain a consistent brand messaging. For example, a business can input a prompt like "Write an email to our subscribers about our new product launch." ChatGPT can then generate an email that includes relevant information about the product launch and encourages subscribers to make a purchase.

Conclusion

ChatGPT is a powerful tool for copywriting and marketing content. It can save businesses time and effort, improve the quality of content, increase productivity, and maintain consistency in tone and style. While ChatGPT is not a substitute for human input, it can significantly enhance the content creation process. With the right prompts and fine-tuning, ChatGPT can generate content that is accurate, engaging, and persuasive, making it an ideal tool for businesses of all sizes.

Introduction

Academic and research writing is a crucial part of higher education and scientific inquiry. It involves the creation of scholarly content that is original, accurate, and informative, and serves to advance knowledge in a particular field of study. Writing academic papers and conducting research is a demanding and time-consuming process that requires extensive research, critical thinking, and analysis. In recent years, the emergence of language models like ChatGPT has revolutionized the way academic and research writing is conducted. This article will discuss how ChatGPT can be used in academic and research writing.

Using ChatGPT for Academic Writing

ChatGPT can be a valuable tool for academic writing, especially for tasks that require large amounts of research and data analysis. Some ways that ChatGPT can be used in academic writing include:

1. Generating Ideas and Outlines

One of the most challenging aspects of academic writing is coming up with ideas and developing an outline for a research paper. ChatGPT can be used to generate ideas and create an outline for a research paper by inputting a topic or research question. ChatGPT can provide relevant research articles, summaries, and keywords that can help researchers develop their ideas and create a structured outline.

2. Summarizing Research Articles

Reading and analyzing research articles is a time-consuming process that requires a significant amount of effort. ChatGPT can be used to summarize research articles, making it easier for researchers to understand the key findings and conclusions without having to read the entire article. This feature can be particularly useful for literature reviews, where researchers need to read and analyze many articles to gather relevant information.

3. Writing Abstracts and Introductions

Abstracts and introductions are essential components of research papers that provide an overview of the research question, methodology, and findings. ChatGPT can be used to generate abstracts and introductions by inputting relevant keywords and data points. This feature can save researchers time and effort by providing a starting point for their writing.

4. Generating References and Citations

One of the most time-consuming aspects of academic writing is creating references and citations for research papers. ChatGPT can be used to generate references and citations in a variety of citation styles, including APA, MLA, and Chicago. This feature can save researchers time and effort by automating the citation process and ensuring that all references are properly formatted.

Using ChatGPT for Research Writing

ChatGPT can also be used for research writing, particularly for tasks that require data analysis and visualization. Some ways that ChatGPT can be used in research writing include:

1. Writing Research Reports

   Research reports are essential components of research studies that provide an overview of the research question, methodology, and findings. ChatGPT can be used to generate research reports by inputting relevant keywords and data points. This feature can save researchers time and effort by providing a starting point for their writing.

2. Writing Research Proposals

   Research proposals are critical documents that outline the scope, methodology, and timeline of a research project. ChatGPT can be used to generate research proposals by inputting relevant keywords and data points. This feature can save researchers time and effort by providing a starting point for their writing and ensuring that all the necessary components of a research proposal are included.

4. Collaborative Writing

   ChatGPT can also be used for collaborative writing by allowing multiple researchers to work on a single document simultaneously. This feature can save researchers time and effort by allowing them to collaborate in real-time and ensuring that all the necessary components of a research paper are included.

Benefits of Using ChatGPT for Academic and Research Writing

Using ChatGPT for academic and research writing has several benefits, including:

1. Time-Saving

ChatGPT can save researchers time by automating tasks like summarizing research articles, generating references and citations, and even writing abstracts and introductions. This feature can help researchers focus on the critical aspects of research, such as data analysis and interpretation.

2. Accuracy

ChatGPT is based on deep learning algorithms that have been trained on a massive corpus of text data, making it an accurate tool for academic and research writing. ChatGPT can provide accurate summaries, citations, and even ideas for research papers, ensuring that researchers have access to high-quality information.

3. Consistency

Using ChatGPT for academic and research writing can also ensure consistency across multiple documents. ChatGPT can generate references and citations in a variety of citation styles, ensuring that all references are formatted consistently.

4. Accessibility

ChatGPT is an accessible tool that can be used by researchers with varying levels of expertise. This feature can help researchers who are new to academic and research writing by providing a starting point for their writing and ensuring that all the necessary components of a research paper are included.

Challenges of Using ChatGPT for Academic and Research Writing

While ChatGPT is a powerful tool for academic and research writing, it also presents some challenges, including:

1. Reliance on Pre-existing Data

ChatGPT is only as good as the data it has been trained on. While ChatGPT has been trained on a massive corpus of text data, it may not have access to specific information or data sets that are relevant to a particular research project.

2. Lack of Contextual Understanding

ChatGPT lacks contextual understanding, which means that it may not be able to recognize the nuances and complexities of a particular research question or topic. This feature can result in ChatGPT providing irrelevant or inaccurate information.

3. Potential for Plagiarism

Using ChatGPT for academic and research writing can also present a potential for plagiarism. Researchers must ensure that they use ChatGPT as a tool and not as a replacement for their critical thinking and analysis.

Conclusion

ChatGPT is a powerful tool that can be used for academic and research writing. It can save researchers time and effort by automating tasks like summarizing research articles, generating references and citations, and even writing abstracts and introductions. ChatGPT can also ensure accuracy, consistency, and accessibility across multiple documents. However, researchers must also be aware of the challenges associated with using ChatGPT, such as reliance on pre-existing data, lack of contextual understanding, and potential for plagiarism. By using ChatGPT as a tool and not as a replacement for their critical thinking and analysis, researchers can harness the power of language models to advance knowledge in their field of study.

Introduction

Fiction and storytelling are an integral part of human culture. From the earliest days of oral traditions to modern-day novels and movies, storytelling has been used to entertain, educate, and inspire people. With the advent of technology, there are new ways to create and tell stories, including using artificial intelligence. One such tool is ChatGPT, a large language model that can generate human-like responses to text prompts. In this article, we will explore how ChatGPT can be used for fiction and storytelling.

Using ChatGPT for Fiction and Storytelling

One of the most exciting applications of ChatGPT is its use in fiction and storytelling. With its ability to generate natural-sounding language, ChatGPT can help writers come up with new ideas and plotlines, or even write entire stories. Here are some ways ChatGPT can be used for fiction and storytelling:

1. Idea Generation

One of the biggest challenges for writers is coming up with new and original ideas for their stories. ChatGPT can help with this by generating prompts and suggestions based on a given theme or genre. For example, if a writer is working on a science fiction story, they could ask ChatGPT for ideas on futuristic technologies or alien species. ChatGPT can provide a wealth of ideas that the writer can then use as inspiration for their own story.

2. Character Creation

Another essential aspect of fiction is creating compelling and believable characters. ChatGPT can help writers with this by generating character profiles based on specific attributes such as personality traits, physical appearance, and backstory. The writer can use these profiles as a starting point for developing their own characters, or even incorporate the generated characters into their story.

3. Plot Development

Once a writer has an idea and characters for their story, the next step is developing the plot. ChatGPT can assist with this by generating plot outlines based on specific genres or themes. For example, if a writer is working on a romance novel, they could ask ChatGPT for plot ideas based on the genre. ChatGPT can provide a variety of plot points and twists that the writer can then incorporate into their story.

4. Dialogue Generation

Dialogue is an essential part of any story, and ChatGPT can help with generating realistic and natural-sounding dialogue. By providing prompts or scenarios, ChatGPT can generate responses that can be used as inspiration for the writer's own dialogue. This can be especially helpful for writers who struggle with writing dialogue or who want to add more depth and realism to their characters' conversations.

5. Story Generation

One of the most exciting ways ChatGPT can be used for fiction and storytelling is by generating entire stories. By providing a prompt or theme, ChatGPT can generate a story from beginning to end. While the generated story may not be perfect, it can provide a starting point for the writer to develop their own story. Additionally, ChatGPT can generate multiple story variations based on the same prompt, providing the writer with a range of options to choose from.

Challenges and Limitations

While ChatGPT can be a powerful tool for fiction and storytelling, there are some challenges and limitations to consider. Here are a few:

1. Lack of Creativity

While ChatGPT can generate a wide range of ideas and storylines, it is limited by the data it was trained on. As a result, it may struggle to come up with truly unique and creative ideas that have not been seen before. It is important for writers to use ChatGPT as a starting point and not rely solely on its suggestions for their entire story.

2. Lack of Contextual Understanding

ChatGPT does not have a true understanding of the context or emotions behind the text prompts it is given. This can result in responses that are not entirely relevant or do not fully capture the intended tone or emotion. It is important for writers to carefully consider the prompts they provide to ChatGPT and use their own judgement when incorporating the generated responses into their stories.

As with any machine learning model, there is the potential for bias in ChatGPT's responses. This is because the model was trained on data that may contain biases or stereotypes, which can be unintentionally replicated in its generated responses. It is important for writers to be aware of this potential and take steps to mitigate it, such as by providing diverse prompts and checking the generated responses for any potentially harmful language.

Conclusion

ChatGPT is a powerful tool that can be used for a variety of natural language processing tasks, including fiction and storytelling. Its ability to generate natural-sounding language and provide ideas and plot points can be incredibly helpful for writers looking for inspiration or struggling with writer's block. However, it is important to remember that ChatGPT is not a substitute for human creativity and judgement. Writers should use it as a tool to enhance their own writing and storytelling abilities, rather than rely on it entirely. With careful consideration and proper use, ChatGPT can be a valuable asset in the writer's toolbox.

Introduction

As e-commerce continues to grow, the importance of product descriptions cannot be overstated. A well-written product description can be the difference between a customer making a purchase or moving on to a competitor's site. This is where ChatGPT, a powerful language model based on the GPT-3.5 architecture, comes in. In this article, we will explore how ChatGPT can be used to generate high-quality product descriptions.

Using ChatGPT for generating product descriptions

Generating product descriptions can be a time-consuming and challenging task, particularly for businesses with a large number of products. ChatGPT can be used to streamline this process and generate high-quality product descriptions quickly and efficiently. Here are some of the ways in which ChatGPT can be used to generate product descriptions:

1. Keyword-based prompts

One way to use ChatGPT for generating product descriptions is by providing it with a set of keywords related to the product. These keywords can be used as a prompt for ChatGPT, which can then generate a description that includes the relevant features and benefits of the product. For example, if the keywords "wireless headphones" are provided, ChatGPT can generate a description that includes details about the product's sound quality, battery life, and compatibility with different devices.

2. Product comparisons

Another way to use ChatGPT for generating product descriptions is by providing it with a set of products to compare. ChatGPT can then generate a description that highlights the similarities and differences between the products, helping customers make an informed decision. For example, if a customer is deciding between two different smartphones, ChatGPT can generate a description that compares their features, such as camera quality, battery life, and screen size.

3. Customized descriptions

ChatGPT can also be used to generate customized product descriptions based on the customer's preferences and needs. By collecting data about the customer's browsing history, previous purchases, and demographic information, businesses can create personalized prompts for ChatGPT. ChatGPT can then generate descriptions that are tailored to the customer's interests, making the shopping experience more engaging and relevant.

Benefits of using ChatGPT for generating product descriptions

1. Time-saving

Generating product descriptions manually can be a time-consuming process, particularly for businesses with a large number of products. ChatGPT can generate high-quality descriptions quickly and efficiently, freeing up time for businesses to focus on other aspects of their operations.

2. Consistency

By using ChatGPT to generate product descriptions, businesses can ensure that the tone and style of the descriptions are consistent across all products. This can help to create a cohesive brand identity and improve the customer experience.

3. Improved SEO

Product descriptions are an essential component of SEO, as they can help to improve a website's search engine ranking. By using ChatGPT to generate descriptions that include relevant keywords and phrases, businesses can improve their SEO and attract more customers to their site.

4. Engaging content

ChatGPT can generate descriptions that are engaging and informative for customers, helping them make an informed decision about the product. This can lead to higher conversion rates and increased customer satisfaction.

5. Scalability

As businesses grow and add more products to their inventory, generating product descriptions manually can become increasingly challenging. ChatGPT can be used to generate descriptions for thousands of products, making it a scalable solution for businesses of all sizes.

6. Cost-effective

Hiring copywriters to generate product descriptions can be expensive, particularly for small businesses. ChatGPT provides a cost-effective solution for businesses that want to generate high-quality descriptions without breaking the bank.

Limitations of using ChatGPT for generating product descriptions

While ChatGPT is a powerful tool for generating product descriptions, it is not without its limitations. Here are some of the potential drawbacks to using ChatGPT for this purpose:

1. Lack of human touch

While ChatGPT can generate descriptions that are indistinguishable from those written by humans, they lack the human touch that can make a description truly compelling. Some customers may prefer descriptions that are written by humans and that include personal anecdotes or other elements that make the product more relatable.

2. Limited creativity

While ChatGPT can generate descriptions based on a set of keywords or other input, it may lack the creativity and originality that can make a description stand out. Copywriters are often able to come up with unique angles and perspectives that can make a product more appealing to customers.

3. Language limitations

While ChatGPT is capable of generating descriptions in multiple languages, it may not be able to capture the nuances and cultural references that can make a description more effective. For businesses that operate in multiple countries, it may be necessary to hire local copywriters to generate descriptions that are tailored to the local market.

4. Quality control

While ChatGPT is capable of generating high-quality descriptions, it may occasionally produce errors or inaccuracies. Businesses will need to implement a system for quality control to ensure that the descriptions generated by ChatGPT are accurate and meet their standards.

Conclusion

ChatGPT is a powerful tool that can be used to generate high-quality product descriptions quickly and efficiently. By providing ChatGPT with keywords or other input, businesses can generate descriptions that are consistent, engaging, and informative. While ChatGPT has its limitations, it provides a cost-effective and scalable solution for businesses that want to generate high-quality product descriptions without hiring copywriters. As e-commerce continues to grow, ChatGPT will become an increasingly valuable tool for businesses that want to stand out in a crowded marketplace.

Chapter 9. Creating chatbot conversations with ChatGPT

Introduction

Chatbots have been around for quite some time, and they are rapidly becoming a popular tool for businesses of all sizes. A chatbot is a computer program designed to simulate conversation with human users, especially over the internet. A chatbot is powered by artificial intelligence, machine learning, and natural language processing technology. Chatbots are being used by businesses to automate customer support, marketing, and even sales. With the rise of chatbots, creating chatbot conversations has become more critical than ever. This article will provide you with a step-by-step guide on how to create chatbot conversations with ChatGPT.

ChatGPT is a language model developed by OpenAI. It is based on the GPT-3.5 architecture and has been trained on a massive dataset of text from the internet. ChatGPT is capable of understanding and generating human-like responses to natural language queries. ChatGPT has been used to develop chatbots for various applications, including customer support, education, and entertainment.

Step 1: Define the purpose of your chatbot

The first step in creating a chatbot conversation with ChatGPT is to define the purpose of your chatbot. What do you want your chatbot to accomplish? Do you want your chatbot to provide customer support, generate leads, or entertain your customers? The purpose of your chatbot will determine the type of conversation you need to create.

Step 2: Determine the persona of your chatbot

The next step is to determine the persona of your chatbot. A persona is the character or identity that your chatbot will adopt when interacting with users. Your chatbot's persona will influence the tone and style of the conversation. You can choose to make your chatbot sound professional, casual, or even humorous, depending on the purpose of your chatbot and the type of audience you are targeting.

Step 3: Create a conversation flowchart

Once you have defined the purpose and persona of your chatbot, the next step is to create a conversation flowchart. A conversation flowchart is a visual representation of the conversation between the chatbot and the user. The flowchart outlines the questions that the chatbot will ask and the responses that it will generate based on the user's input. Creating a conversation flowchart will help you to organize your conversation and ensure that it flows logically.

Step 4: Generate responses with ChatGPT

After creating a conversation flowchart, you can start generating responses with ChatGPT. ChatGPT can generate responses to user queries in natural language, making it an excellent tool for creating chatbot conversations. To generate responses with ChatGPT, you need to input the user's query into the system and wait for the response. ChatGPT will analyze the user's input and generate a response based on its understanding of the query.

Step 5: Test your chatbot conversation

Once you have generated responses with ChatGPT, the next step is to test your chatbot conversation. Testing your chatbot conversation will help you to identify any issues and make improvements. You can test your chatbot conversation by simulating conversations between the chatbot and users. You can also get feedback from users to improve the quality of the conversation.

Step 6: Train your chatbot

Training your chatbot is an essential step in improving the quality of the conversation. ChatGPT is a machine learning model that can learn from the conversations it has with users. You can use the conversations you have with users to train your chatbot to generate better responses. You can also use feedback from users to improve the quality of your chatbot conversation.

Step 7: Deploy your chatbot

Once you have tested and trained your chatbot, the final step is to deploy it. You can deploy your chatbot on various platforms, including your website, social media platforms, and messaging apps. You can also integrate your chatbot with other tools, such as CRM software and marketing automation tools, to improve its functionality.

Tips for Creating Chatbot Conversations with ChatGPT

Here are some tips to keep in mind when creating chatbot conversations with ChatGPT:

1. Keep it simple: The conversation between the chatbot and the user should be simple and easy to understand. Avoid using technical terms and jargon that the user may not understand.

2. Be conversational: Your chatbot should sound like a human and not a machine. Use conversational language and avoid sounding too formal or robotic.

3. Personalize the conversation: Personalize the conversation by using the user's name and other personal information. This will make the conversation more engaging and increase the user's satisfaction.

4. Use emojis: Emojis can be used to express emotions and add a personal touch to the conversation. However, use them sparingly and only when appropriate.

5. Use images and videos: Images and videos can be used to enhance the conversation and provide visual aids. Use them when necessary to make the conversation more engaging.

6. Be responsive: Your chatbot should respond quickly to the user's queries. Slow response times can lead to frustration and a negative user experience.

7. Provide value: Your chatbot should provide value to the user by solving their problems, answering their questions, and providing helpful information.

Conclusion

Creating chatbot conversations with ChatGPT can be an effective way to automate customer support, marketing, and sales. By following the steps outlined in this article and keeping these tips in mind, you can create engaging and effective chatbot conversations with ChatGPT. Remember to define the purpose and persona of your chatbot, create a conversation flowchart, generate responses with ChatGPT, test and train your chatbot, and deploy it on various platforms. With ChatGPT, you can create chatbot conversations that are natural, engaging, and effective in achieving your business objectives.

Chapter 10. ChatGPT for generating video scripts and ideas

Introduction

In recent years, the entertainment industry has seen a surge in demand for video content across various platforms, including social media, streaming services, and traditional media. As a result, creators are under pressure to generate new ideas and engaging scripts that resonate with their target audience. This is where ChatGPT comes in - a powerful tool that can assist creators in generating video scripts and ideas quickly and efficiently.

ChatGPT is a large language model based on the GPT-3.5 architecture that has been trained on an enormous corpus of text data, including books, articles, and websites. Its primary function is to generate natural language responses to user queries, making it an excellent tool for generating video scripts and ideas.

ChatGPT works by using a process called deep learning, where it analyzes the context of the user's input and generates a response based on that context. It is designed to understand natural language and can generate responses that are similar to those written by a human. Users can input a prompt or a question related to their video content, and ChatGPT will generate a script or idea based on that input.

Benefits of using ChatGPT for video content creation

1. Time-Saving

Generating ideas and scripts can be a time-consuming process for creators, taking away from their other important tasks. With ChatGPT, creators can generate ideas and scripts quickly, allowing them to focus on other aspects of their video production process.

2. Creative Inspiration

Sometimes, creators may find themselves stuck when it comes to generating new and creative ideas. ChatGPT can help provide inspiration by generating unique and exciting concepts that creators may not have thought of otherwise.

3. Consistency

One of the most significant advantages of using ChatGPT is the ability to maintain consistency in the tone and style of the content. ChatGPT generates responses based on the user's input, ensuring that the content remains on-brand and consistent.

4. Personalization

ChatGPT can be personalized to a user's specific needs, making it an excellent tool for creators looking to generate content in a specific niche or industry.

How to use ChatGPT for video content creation

1. Start with a prompt or question

To use ChatGPT effectively, creators should start with a clear prompt or question related to their video content. This could be a general topic, specific theme, or a particular character or scenario.

2. Choose the appropriate model

ChatGPT offers several models with different capabilities and levels of complexity. Creators should choose a model that is appropriate for their needs, depending on the level of detail and specificity required.

3. Refine the output

Once ChatGPT generates a response, creators can refine the output by adjusting the length, tone, and other parameters to fit their specific requirements.

4. Edit and finalize the script

While ChatGPT can generate scripts quickly and efficiently, it is still important for creators to review and edit the content to ensure it meets their standards and aligns with their vision for the video content.

Examples of how ChatGPT can be used for video content creation

1. Generating video ideas

ChatGPT can be used to generate unique and engaging video ideas for creators in various industries. For example, a travel vlogger can input a prompt related to a specific destination or activity, and ChatGPT can generate ideas for unique experiences, hidden gems, and local attractions to feature in the vlog.

2. Scriptwriting

ChatGPT can be used to generate scripts for various types of video content, including short films, web series, and promotional videos. For example, a creator can input a prompt related to a specific character or scenario, and ChatGPT can generate a script that fits the theme and tone of the video.

3. Dialogue and character development

ChatGPT can be used to generate dialogue for characters in a video, as well as develop their personality traits and backstory. For example, a creator can input a prompt related to a specific character in their video, and ChatGPT can generate dialogue that fits the character's personality and aligns with the overall theme of the video.

4. Marketing and promotion

ChatGPT can be used to generate copy for video titles, descriptions, and social media posts to promote the video content. For example, a creator can input a prompt related to the video content and its target audience, and ChatGPT can generate copy that is engaging, informative, and aligned with the brand's voice and tone.

Limitations of using ChatGPT for video content creation

1. Lack of creativity

While ChatGPT can generate unique and engaging ideas, it may not always provide the level of creativity required for some video content. Creators may still need to rely on their creativity and experience to generate truly unique and compelling content.

2. Accuracy and specificity

ChatGPT may not always generate responses that are accurate or specific enough for the user's needs. Creators may need to adjust the output or input more specific prompts to generate the level of detail required for their video content.

3. Machine bias

As with any machine learning model, ChatGPT may have biases based on the data it was trained on. Creators should be aware of these biases and take steps to ensure that their video content is inclusive and representative of all audiences.

Conclusion

ChatGPT is a powerful tool that can assist creators in generating video scripts and ideas quickly and efficiently. Its ability to understand natural language and generate responses similar to those written by a human makes it an excellent choice for creators looking to streamline their video content creation process. However, creators should also be aware of its limitations and take steps to ensure that their video content is creative, accurate, and inclusive. Overall, ChatGPT can be a valuable tool for creators in various industries looking to generate engaging and compelling video content.

Introduction

In today's globalized world, businesses are operating on a global scale. One of the significant challenges they face is communicating effectively with customers who speak different languages. Localization and translation are crucial for businesses to establish a strong international presence. In recent years, advances in Artificial Intelligence (AI) have led to the development of sophisticated language models like ChatGPT, which can be used for content localization and translation.

In this article, we will explore how businesses can use ChatGPT for content localization and translation. We will discuss the benefits of using ChatGPT, its limitations, and the best practices for using it effectively.

Benefits of using ChatGPT for content localization and translation

1. High accuracy: ChatGPT is highly accurate in translating text from one language to another. The model has been trained on a massive corpus of text, making it highly effective in recognizing and translating words and phrases accurately.

2. Fast: ChatGPT can translate text at lightning-fast speed. This is because the model has been optimized to process large amounts of text quickly.

3. Cost-effective: ChatGPT is a cost-effective solution for businesses looking to localize and translate their content. Compared to human translators, ChatGPT can work 24/7 without breaks, making it a cost-effective solution for businesses.

4. Scalable: ChatGPT is highly scalable, making it suitable for businesses of all sizes. Whether you are a small business or a large enterprise, ChatGPT can handle your content localization and translation needs.

Limitations of using ChatGPT for content localization and translation

1. Cultural nuances: ChatGPT may not be able to capture cultural nuances accurately, which can be a significant limitation in content localization. For instance, certain words or phrases may have different connotations in different cultures, which ChatGPT may not be able to capture accurately.

2. Language limitations: ChatGPT can only translate between languages that it has been trained on. Therefore, if you need to translate text into a language that ChatGPT has not been trained on, you may need to consider other translation options.

3. Accuracy issues: While ChatGPT is highly accurate, it is not perfect. There may be instances where the model produces inaccurate translations or fails to capture the meaning of a text accurately.

Best practices for using ChatGPT for content localization and translation

1. Provide context: Providing context is crucial for ensuring accurate translations. When using ChatGPT for content localization and translation, it is essential to provide as much context as possible to ensure that the model can capture the meaning of the text accurately.

2. Edit translations: While ChatGPT is highly accurate, it is always a good idea to have a human editor review the translations. This can help catch any inaccuracies or mistakes that the model may have missed.

3. Use multiple models: It is a good practice to use multiple language models when translating content. This can help ensure that the translations are accurate and capture the nuances of the language.

4. Train the model: If you are using ChatGPT to translate content for a specific industry or domain, it may be worthwhile to train the model on industry-specific terminology. This can help ensure that the model produces accurate translations that are specific to your industry.

Conclusion

ChatGPT is a powerful tool for businesses looking to localize and translate their content. Its high accuracy, speed, cost-effectiveness, and scalability make it a popular choice for businesses of all sizes. However, it is important to keep in mind its limitations, particularly in capturing cultural nuances and accuracy issues.

To use ChatGPT effectively for content localization and translation, it is essential to provide context, edit translations, use multiple models, and train the model for specific industries or domains. By following these best practices, businesses can ensure that their content is accurately translated and localized for their target audience.

In conclusion, ChatGPT has revolutionized the field of content localization and translation, providing businesses with a fast, accurate, and cost-effective solution. While it may not be perfect, it is a valuable tool that can help businesses establish a strong international presence and communicate effectively with their customers in different languages. As AI technology continues to evolve, we can expect to see even more sophisticated language models that will further enhance content localization and translation in the future.

Introduction

The advancement of Artificial Intelligence has led to the emergence of natural language processing models, which have helped revolutionize several industries. Among the natural language processing models is the GPT-3, an advanced deep learning model developed by OpenAI. ChatGPT is an extension of the GPT-3 model, designed to interact with users by generating text-based responses.

One of the most significant advantages of ChatGPT is its ability to generate news headlines and articles. With ChatGPT, news agencies can significantly reduce the time it takes to produce news content. Additionally, ChatGPT can analyze large volumes of data and produce concise, accurate, and informative news articles.

This article will explore how ChatGPT can generate news headlines and articles and the benefits of using ChatGPT for news content creation.

How ChatGPT Works for News Content Generation

ChatGPT utilizes deep learning algorithms to generate news headlines and articles. The model is trained on a large corpus of data, which includes news articles, blog posts, and other textual content. The training data is used to create a neural network that can recognize patterns and generate responses to specific prompts.

When generating news headlines and articles, ChatGPT analyzes the input prompt and generates a response based on the patterns it has learned from the training data. This is how language models like ChatGPT work - they use statistical patterns learned from large amounts of data to generate new text based on a given prompt or context.

For instance, if the input prompt is "Breaking News: Earthquake in California," ChatGPT could potentially generate a headline such as "7.5 Magnitude Earthquake Hits California, Several Injured." However, it's important to note that the quality and accuracy of the generated headline would depend on various factors, including the quality of the training data, the complexity of the prompt, and the specific configuration of the language model.

As an AI language model, ChatGPT does not have direct access to live news feeds or data sources. However, it is possible for ChatGPT to provide news updates on specific topics by analyzing news articles and other sources of information. This would require a user to input a specific topic or keyword related to the news they are interested in, and ChatGPT would then generate a response based on the patterns it has learned from the training data.

The Benefits of Using ChatGPT for News Content Creation

1. Speed and Efficiency: ChatGPT can generate news headlines and articles in real-time. This is particularly useful for breaking news events that require immediate coverage. News agencies can use ChatGPT to generate headlines and articles within seconds, eliminating the need for journalists to spend hours researching and writing news content.

2. Accurate and Informative: ChatGPT can analyze vast amounts of data and produce accurate and informative news articles. The model can process large volumes of data in a short time and identify relevant information that can be included in the article. Additionally, ChatGPT can generate articles that are free from human biases, ensuring that the content is objective and unbiased.

3. Consistency: ChatGPT can produce consistent and high-quality news articles. The model is trained on a large corpus of data, which ensures that the output is consistent across all articles. Additionally, ChatGPT can generate articles that adhere to a specific writing style, ensuring that the content is consistent with the publication's brand and tone.

4. Cost-Effective: ChatGPT can significantly reduce the cost of news content creation. News agencies can use ChatGPT to generate news articles and headlines, eliminating the need for additional journalists and reducing the overall cost of news production.

ChatGPT for Personalized News Delivery

ChatGPT can also be used for personalized news delivery. The model can analyze user preferences and generate news content tailored to their interests. This is particularly useful for news agencies that want to offer a personalized news experience to their readers.

ChatGPT can analyze user behavior and generate news content based on their reading habits. For instance, if a user frequently reads articles about technology, ChatGPT can generate news articles related to technology that the user is likely to find interesting.

Personalized news delivery can help news agencies increase user engagement and retain readers. By offering personalized news content, news agencies can provide users with a more tailored and relevant news experience, leading to higher user engagement and retention rates.

Limitations of ChatGPT for News Content Generation

While ChatGPT has several benefits for news content generation, there are also limitations that need to be considered. Some of the limitations include:

1. Lack of Contextual Understanding: ChatGPT can generate headlines and articles based on patterns it has learned from the training data. However, the model may not fully understand the context of the news event, leading to inaccuracies or incomplete information in the article.

2. Inability to Conduct Interviews: ChatGPT cannot conduct interviews or gather information from sources. While the model can analyze data from various sources, it cannot verify the accuracy of the information, leading to potential inaccuracies in the article.

3. Dependence on Training Data: ChatGPT's ability to generate accurate news content is dependent on the quality of the training data. If the training data is biased or inaccurate, the model's output may also be biased or inaccurate.

4. Lack of Creativity: ChatGPT can generate news content based on patterns it has learned from the training data. However, the model may lack the creativity and

originality that human journalists can bring to news content creation.

Conclusion

ChatGPT is an advanced natural language processing model that can generate news headlines and articles. The model's ability to analyze vast amounts of data and produce accurate and informative news content in real-time has significant benefits for news agencies. ChatGPT can help news agencies reduce the time and cost of news content creation, while also providing consistent and high-quality news articles.

Additionally, ChatGPT can be used for personalized news delivery, providing users with a more tailored and relevant news experience. However, it is important to note that ChatGPT has limitations, including its lack of contextual understanding, inability to conduct interviews, dependence on training data, and lack of creativity.

Overall, ChatGPT has the potential to revolutionize the news industry by providing news agencies with a powerful tool for news content generation. As the technology continues to evolve, it will be interesting to see how ChatGPT and other natural language processing models shape the future of news content creation.

Chapter 13. ChatGPT for generating speech transcripts and summaries

Introduction

The ability to transcribe and summarize speech is becoming increasingly important in various fields, including journalism, research, law, and education. However, manually transcribing and summarizing speech can be time-consuming and resource-intensive. Fortunately, recent advancements in natural language processing (NLP) have made it possible to automate the process of generating speech transcripts and summaries. One such NLP model is ChatGPT, a language model developed by OpenAI that has shown impressive performance in a variety of natural language tasks, including speech transcription and summarization.

In this article, we will explore the capabilities of ChatGPT in generating speech transcripts and summaries, and discuss its potential applications in various fields.

How ChatGPT Can Be Used for Speech Transcription

Speech transcription is the process of converting spoken words into written text. This can be a time-consuming and labor-intensive task, especially for long speeches or interviews. ChatGPT can be used to automate the process of speech transcription, making it faster and more efficient. To use ChatGPT for speech transcription, the audio of the speech is first converted into a text format, such as a transcript or closed captions. This text is then fed into the ChatGPT model, which generates a more accurate and complete transcription of the speech.

One of the advantages of using ChatGPT for speech transcription is its ability to capture context and nuance. Unlike traditional speech recognition software, which relies on pre-defined rules and statistical models, ChatGPT can understand the meaning behind the words and generate text that is more accurate and relevant.

How ChatGPT Can Be Used for Speech Summarization

Speech summarization is the process of condensing a long speech or presentation into a shorter, more concise summary. This can be useful for a variety of applications, such as news reporting, academic research, and legal proceedings. ChatGPT can be used to automate the process of speech summarization, making it faster and more efficient.

To use ChatGPT for speech summarization, the audio of the speech is first converted into a text format, such as a transcript or closed captions. This text is then fed into the ChatGPT model, which generates a summary of the speech that captures the most important points and themes.

One of the advantages of using ChatGPT for speech summarization is its ability to identify and prioritize the most relevant information. Unlike traditional summarization techniques, which rely on simple heuristics or statistical models, ChatGPT can understand the context and meaning behind the words and generate summaries that are more accurate and informative.

Applications of ChatGPT in Speech Transcription and Summarization

ChatGPT has the potential to be used in a variety of fields and applications that require speech transcription and summarization. Some potential applications include:

1. Journalism: ChatGPT can be used to automatically generate transcripts and summaries of speeches and press conferences, making it easier and faster for journalists to report on important events.

2. Research: ChatGPT can be used to transcribe and summarize interviews and focus groups for qualitative research studies. This can save researchers time and resources, and also ensure that important information is not missed during the transcription process.

3. Education: ChatGPT can be used to transcribe and summarize lectures and presentations for students, making it easier for them to review and study the material. This can be particularly helpful for students who may have difficulty taking notes during lectures or who need to review material in a shorter amount of time.

4. Legal proceedings: ChatGPT can be used to transcribe and summarize court proceedings and depositions, making it easier for lawyers and judges to review important testimony and evidence.

5. Business: ChatGPT can be used to transcribe and summarize business meetings and presentations, making it easier for employees to review and remember key points and action items.

Challenges and Limitations of ChatGPT in Speech Transcription and Summarization

While ChatGPT shows promise in generating speech transcripts and summaries, there are still some challenges and limitations that need to be addressed.

One of the main challenges is the quality of the input data. ChatGPT relies on accurate and comprehensive transcripts or closed captions to generate accurate transcriptions and summaries. If the input data is incomplete or inaccurate, the output generated by ChatGPT may also be incomplete or inaccurate.

Another challenge is the bias in the input data. ChatGPT is trained on a large corpus of text data, which may contain biases and inaccuracies that are reflected in the output generated by the model. This can be particularly problematic in fields such as journalism and research, where accurate and unbiased reporting is critical.

Finally, there is a limitation in the length of the input data that can be processed by ChatGPT. The model is designed to process sequences of up to a certain length, and longer sequences may need to be split into smaller segments for processing.

Conclusion

ChatGPT is a powerful tool for generating speech transcripts and summaries, and has the potential to be used in a wide range of applications in various fields. Its ability to capture context and nuance makes it a valuable tool for speech transcription and summarization, and its high level of fluency and coherence ensures that the output generated by the model is accurate and relevant. However, there are still challenges and limitations that need to be addressed, particularly with regards to the quality and bias of the input data. Overall, ChatGPT represents a significant advancement in the field of natural language processing and has the potential to revolutionize the way we generate speech transcripts and summaries.

Introduction

In today's fast-paced digital world, content curation and aggregation have become crucial skills for anyone who wants to stay informed and up-to-date with the latest news and trends. With the overwhelming amount of information available on the internet, it can be challenging to filter through all the noise and find the most relevant and valuable content. Fortunately, with the rise of artificial intelligence and natural language processing, tools like ChatGPT have emerged to make content curation and aggregation easier and more efficient than ever before.

Using ChatGPT for content curation and aggregation

One of the most useful applications of ChatGPT is content curation and aggregation. With ChatGPT, you can easily gather information from a variety of sources, filter out irrelevant or low-quality content, and present the most valuable and relevant content to your audience. Here are some tips for using ChatGPT for content curation and aggregation:

1. Set up your criteria

Before you start using ChatGPT for content curation and aggregation, you need to define your criteria. What topics are you interested in? What types of content do you want to curate and aggregate? What sources do you want to include or exclude? Once you have a clear understanding of your criteria, you can start training ChatGPT to find the content that meets your needs.

2. Use ChatGPT to search for content

Once you have your criteria in place, you can start using ChatGPT to search for content. For example, you can ask ChatGPT to search for blog posts or articles that meet your criteria. ChatGPT can also search for content on social media platforms like Twitter or Reddit, which can be a great way to discover new content and stay up-to-date with the latest trends.

3. Filter out irrelevant content

Once ChatGPT has found a list of potential content, you need to filter out any irrelevant or low-quality content. ChatGPT can help with this by analyzing the content and identifying keywords, topics, and other criteria that match your search criteria. You can also train ChatGPT to recognize certain sources as high-quality or low-quality, which can help it filter out content that is not worth curating or aggregating.

4. Present the curated content

Once you have filtered out the irrelevant content, you can present the curated content to your audience. This can be done in a variety of ways, depending on your goals and audience. For example, you can create a newsletter that includes a summary of the most important news and trends in your industry, or you can create a social media account that shares links to the most valuable and relevant content on a particular topic.

Benefits of using ChatGPT for content curation and aggregation

There are several benefits to using ChatGPT for content curation and aggregation:

1. Time-saving

One of the biggest benefits of using ChatGPT for content curation and aggregation is that it can save you time. Instead of manually searching for content and filtering out irrelevant content, ChatGPT can do the work for you. This means you can spend more time creating valuable content and engaging with your audience, rather than searching for content.

2. Accuracy

ChatGPT is incredibly accurate at identifying and analyzing content. This means you can trust it to find the most relevant and valuable content on a particular topic, without having to spend hours manually sifting through search results. This accuracy is thanks to its advanced natural language processing capabilities, which allow it to understand context and meaning in a way that other search engines cannot.

3. Customization

Another benefit of using ChatGPT for content curation and aggregation is the ability to customize your search criteria. This means you can fine-tune your search to find the exact type of content you are looking for, and exclude sources or topics that are not relevant to your needs. This customization can save you time and ensure that the content you curate and aggregate is of high quality and relevance to your audience.

4. Scalability

Using ChatGPT for content curation and aggregation also allows you to scale your efforts. Whether you are curating content for a small audience or a large one, ChatGPT can help you find the content you need and present it in a way that is engaging and valuable to your audience. This scalability means you can grow your content curation and aggregation efforts over time, without sacrificing quality or efficiency.

Best practices for using ChatGPT for content curation and aggregation

To get the most out of ChatGPT for content curation and aggregation, there are some best practices to keep in mind:

1. Train ChatGPT regularly

To ensure that ChatGPT is finding the most relevant and valuable content for your needs, it is important to train it regularly. This means refining your search criteria, adding new sources, and adjusting its filters as needed. By training ChatGPT regularly, you can ensure that it is always up-to-date and providing the best content for your audience.

2. Use multiple sources

While ChatGPT is great at finding and analyzing content, it is important to use multiple sources to ensure that you are getting a well-rounded view of a particular topic. This means including sources from different viewpoints and perspectives, and not relying solely on one source or type of content.

3. Check for accuracy

While ChatGPT is incredibly accurate, it is still important to check for accuracy when curating and aggregating content. This means fact-checking and verifying sources before sharing them with your audience. By taking the time to ensure that the content you share is accurate and reliable, you can build trust with your audience and establish yourself as a valuable source of information.

4. Add your own commentary

Finally, it is important to add your own commentary and perspective to the content you curate and aggregate. This can help your audience understand why the content is important and how it relates to their lives and interests. By adding your own insights and perspective, you can also establish yourself as a thought leader in your industry and build a strong relationship with your audience.

Conclusion

Using ChatGPT for content curation and aggregation is a powerful tool that can save you time, improve accuracy, and provide valuable content to your audience. By setting up your criteria, using ChatGPT to search for content, filtering out irrelevant content, and presenting the curated content to your audience, you can create a valuable resource for your audience and establish yourself as a thought leader in your industry. With regular training and attention to accuracy and customization, ChatGPT can be a valuable asset for any content curator or aggregator looking to stay on top of the latest news and trends.

Chapter 15. ChatGPT for generating technical documentation

Introduction

Generating technical documentation can be a challenging task, requiring a lot of time and effort to accurately convey information to readers. However, with the advancement of artificial intelligence, this process can now be simplified with the use of ChatGPT, a large language model trained by OpenAI, based on the GPT-3.5 architecture. ChatGPT can assist in generating technical documentation that is clear, concise, and comprehensive, saving both time and resources for businesses and individuals.

How can ChatGPT help generate technical documentation?

ChatGPT can be a valuable tool for generating technical documentation, such as user manuals, product specifications, and technical reports. Here are some ways in which ChatGPT can help:

1. Streamlining the documentation process

One of the biggest advantages of using ChatGPT for technical documentation is that it can significantly reduce the time and resources needed for the documentation process. With ChatGPT, you can quickly generate accurate and comprehensive text without having to spend time researching, drafting, and revising. This can be particularly beneficial for businesses that need to produce a large volume of technical documentation in a short amount of time.

2. Ensuring accuracy and consistency

Another advantage of using ChatGPT for technical documentation is that it can help ensure accuracy and consistency in the text. ChatGPT uses advanced algorithms and natural language processing techniques to understand the context and intent behind the text and generate relevant and accurate content. This can help reduce the risk of errors or inconsistencies that may occur when writing technical documentation manually.

3. Improving readability and user experience

Technical documentation can often be dense and difficult to understand for the average reader. ChatGPT can help improve the readability and user experience of technical documentation by generating text that is clear, concise, and easy to understand. This can be particularly important for businesses that want to ensure that their users can quickly and easily understand how to use their products or services.

4. Personalizing the documentation

ChatGPT can also be used to personalize technical documentation to specific audiences or contexts. For example, if you are creating a user manual for a particular product, ChatGPT can generate text that is tailored to the specific features and functions of that product. This can help improve the user experience and make the documentation more relevant and engaging for the reader.

5. Scaling the documentation

Finally, ChatGPT can help scale the documentation process by generating text in multiple languages. This can be particularly useful for businesses that operate globally and need to create technical documentation in multiple languages. ChatGPT can generate accurate and relevant content in a wide range of languages, saving time and resources for businesses.

Limitations of ChatGPT for technical documentation

While ChatGPT can be a valuable tool for generating technical documentation, it is important to note that it does have some limitations. Here are some of the main limitations to keep in mind:

1. Lack of domain-specific knowledge

One of the main limitations of ChatGPT for technical documentation is that it lacks domain-specific knowledge. While ChatGPT can generate accurate and relevant text based on the input data, it may not have the same level of expertise or understanding as a human expert in a particular field. This can be particularly problematic for highly technical or specialized topics that require a deep understanding of a particular subject area.

2. Need for training data

Another limitation of ChatGPT is that it requires a large amount of training data to generate accurate and relevant text. This means that businesses or individuals who want to use ChatGPT for technical documentation may need to provide a large amount of data to train the model. This can be time-consuming and costly, especially for businesses that need to generate technical documentation for a wide range of products or services.

3. Potential for errors and biases

While ChatGPT is designed to generate accurate and relevant text, there is still the potential for errors and biases to occur. For example, if the training data used to train the model is biased, this bias can be reflected in the generated text. Similarly, if the input data is incomplete or inaccurate, this can also result in errors in the generated text.

4. Lack of creativity and nuance

Finally, another limitation of ChatGPT is that it lacks creativity and nuance. While ChatGPT can generate accurate and relevant text based on the input data, it may not be able to generate text that is creative or nuanced in the way that a human writer can. This can be particularly problematic for technical documentation that requires a more creative or persuasive approach.

Best practices for using ChatGPT for technical documentation

To overcome the limitations of ChatGPT for technical documentation, it is important to follow some best practices. Here are some tips to keep in mind when using ChatGPT for technical documentation.

1. Provide high-quality training data

To ensure that ChatGPT generates accurate and relevant text, it is important to provide high-quality training data. This means providing data that is relevant to the specific domain or subject area and is free from errors or biases.

2. Use multiple models

To reduce the risk of errors or biases, it may be useful to use multiple ChatGPT models to generate different sections of the technical documentation. This can help ensure that the generated text is consistent and accurate across all sections.

3. Review and edit the generated text

While ChatGPT can generate accurate and relevant text, it is important to review and edit the generated text to ensure that it is clear, concise, and comprehensive. This can help ensure that the technical documentation is easy to understand and use for the intended audience.

4. Use ChatGPT in conjunction with human writers

To ensure that the technical documentation is accurate and comprehensive, it may be useful to use ChatGPT in conjunction with human writers. This can help ensure that the generated text is accurate and reflects the intended message, while also adding a level of creativity and nuance that ChatGPT may not be able to provide.

Conclusion

ChatGPT can be a valuable tool for generating technical documentation that is clear, concise, and comprehensive. It can help streamline the documentation process, ensure accuracy and consistency, improve readability and user experience, personalize the documentation, and scale the documentation process. However, it is important to keep in mind the limitations of ChatGPT for technical documentation and to follow best practices to ensure that the generated text is accurate and relevant. By doing so, businesses and individuals can save time and resources while still producing high-quality technical documentation.

Introduction

ChatGPT is a language model developed by OpenAI that can generate human-like responses to various prompts. It is an excellent tool for content creation, and many people use it for various purposes, including writing articles, creating social media posts, and responding to emails. While ChatGPT is an excellent tool for content creation, it also raises several ethical considerations that content creators must consider when using it. In this article, we will discuss the ethical considerations when using ChatGPT for content creation.

1. Bias: One of the primary ethical considerations when using ChatGPT for content creation is bias. Like any other machine learning model, ChatGPT is only as good as the data it is trained on. If the data it is trained on is biased, ChatGPT will also be biased. This means that content creators must be aware of the potential for bias when using ChatGPT and take steps to ensure that the data they use is as unbiased as possible. They should also be aware of the biases inherent in the language model itself, as even if the data is unbiased, ChatGPT may still generate biased responses.

2. Misinformation: Another ethical consideration when using ChatGPT for content creation is the potential for misinformation. ChatGPT can generate responses to any prompt, and while it is generally quite good at generating accurate and helpful responses, it is also possible for it to generate responses that are inaccurate

or even intentionally misleading. Content creators must be aware of this potential and take steps to ensure that the responses generated by ChatGPT are as accurate and helpful as possible. They should also be aware of the potential for ChatGPT to generate responses that may be intentionally misleading, particularly if the prompt is designed to elicit a specific response.

3. Ownership: Another ethical consideration when using ChatGPT for content creation is ownership. While ChatGPT generates responses to prompts, the content it generates is still the intellectual property of the content creator who provided the prompt. However, as ChatGPT is a machine learning model, it is possible that the responses it generates may be similar or identical to responses generated by other users. This raises questions about ownership and plagiarism, and content creators must be aware of these issues when using ChatGPT.

4. Transparency: Transparency is another ethical consideration when using ChatGPT for content creation. Content creators must be transparent about the fact that they are using ChatGPT to generate responses. This means that they should disclose the fact that they are using ChatGPT in any content they create using the tool, and they should also be transparent about the limitations of ChatGPT and the potential for bias or misinformation.

5. Consent: Another ethical consideration when using ChatGPT for content creation is consent. If content creators are using ChatGPT to generate responses to prompts from other people, they must ensure that they have obtained the consent of those individuals to use the responses generated by ChatGPT. This means that they should inform those individuals that they are using

ChatGPT to generate responses and obtain their explicit consent before using the responses generated by the tool.

6. Respect: Respect is another important ethical consideration when using ChatGPT for content creation. Content creators must respect the privacy and dignity of the individuals they are creating content for and ensure that the responses generated by ChatGPT are respectful and appropriate. This means that they should avoid using ChatGPT to generate responses that are insulting, offensive, or discriminatory.

7. Accountability: Finally, accountability is an essential ethical consideration when using ChatGPT for content creation. Content creators must be accountable for the responses generated by ChatGPT and must take responsibility for any harm that may result from the use of the tool. This means that they should be transparent about the fact that they are using ChatGPT and take steps to ensure that the responses generated by the tool are as accurate, helpful, and ethical as possible. They should also be prepared to take corrective action if it becomes apparent that the responses generated by ChatGPT are causing harm or are otherwise unethical.

Conclusion

ChatGPT is a powerful tool for content creation, but it also raises several ethical considerations that content creators must consider when using it. Bias, misinformation, ownership, transparency, consent, respect, and accountability are all important ethical considerations that content creators must be aware of when using ChatGPT for content creation. By being aware of these considerations and taking steps to ensure that the responses generated by ChatGPT are as accurate, helpful, and ethical as possible, content creators can use this tool to create high-quality content that is both informative and respectful. Ultimately, the responsible use of ChatGPT for content creation requires careful consideration of these ethical considerations, as well as ongoing monitoring and evaluation of the tool's impact on the content being created.

"Mastering Content Creation with ChatGPT" is an innovative guide that explores the capabilities of ChatGPT, a powerful language model that has revolutionized the field of artificial intelligence. The book is divided into sixteen chapters that cover a wide range of topics related to content creation, including social media, blog writing, email subject lines, copywriting, academic writing, storytelling, product descriptions, chatbot conversations, video scripts, content localization and translation, news headlines, speech transcripts, technical documentation, and content curation. The book also discusses the ethical considerations that should be kept in mind when using ChatGPT for content creation. With practical tips, real-world examples, and step-by-step guides, this book is an essential resource for anyone looking to take their content creation skills to the next level using the power of ChatGPT.

ABOUT THE AUTHOR

Mr. C. P. Kumar is a retired Scientist 'G' from National Institute of Hydrology, Roorkee, Uttarakhand, India. He is also a Reiki Healer and Chakra Balancing practitioner (with pendulum dowsing) and offers Emotional Freedom Technique (EFT) to help individuals with emotional issues. Mr. Kumar has authored many books on technical, spiritual, and social topics.

For further details, you may visit his webpage
https://www.angelfire.com/nh/cpkumar/virgo.html